CH MAY 2008
NA JUL 2011
EN JUN '14

BACK TO BASICS

The Back to Basics series was devised and produced by McRae Books Srl, Borgo S. Croce, 8, Florence (Italy) www.mcraebooks.com

Publishers: Anne McRae and Marco Nardi
Text: Loredana Agosta, Anne McRae
Main Illustrations: Lorenzo Cecchi, Matteo Chesi, Ferruccio Cucchiarini, Inklink, MM comunicazione (Manuela Cappon, Monica Favilli), Francesca D'Ottavi, Paola Ravaglia
Illustrations: Studio Stalio (Alessandro Cantucci, Fabiano Fabbrucci, Margherita Salvadori)
Design: Marco Nardi
Layout: Rebecca Milner
Color separations: Fotolito Toscana, Firenze

© 2008 McRae Books Srl, Florence

All rights reserved. No part of this book may be reproduced, stored in a retrieval system, or transmitted in any form or by any means, electronic, mechanical, photocopying, or otherwise, without the prior written permission of the copyright holder.

Library of Congress Cataloging-in-Publication Data

McRae, Anne.
  Who were the ancient Greeks? / by Anne McRae-Loredana Agosta.
      p. cm. -- (Back to basics)
  Includes index.
   ISBN 978-88-6098-052-6 (alk. paper)
 1. Greece--Civilization--To 146 B.C. I. Title.
DF77.M37 2007
938--dc22
                                            2007006124

Printed and bound in Malaysia.

Back to Basics

ANCIENT GREECE

McRae Books

Warriors and War see page 20

Greek Colonies see page 13

Contents

Who were the Ancient Greeks?	6–7		
Before the Greeks	8–9	Food and Farming	26–27
Archaic Times	10–11	Clothing and Jewelry	28–29
Greek Colonies	12–13	Trade and Influence	30–31
Classical Greece	14–15	Index	32
Religion	16–17		
Art and Architecture	18–19		
Warriors and War	20–21		
Theater and Entertainment	22-23		
Knowledge	24–25		

Art and Architecture see page 19

Food and Farming see page 27

✳ **Homer**
see page 10

Musicians, like the one shown here, traveled from town to town to entertain the people with stories and songs about the gods and goddesses or great battles and heroic warriors.

Government

It was the Greeks who gave us both the word and the idea for democracy. They developed a system in which citizens could take part in government and vote on how their city state should be run.

✳ **Classical Greece**
see pages 14–15

This scene shows the market place in the city of Athens. Of all the Greek cities we know most about Athens because so much of what happened there was recorded and has survived to the present.

Knowledge

Many aspects of modern life have roots in ancient Greek learning and culture. The Greeks practically invented many fields of study, such as history and philosophy, and introduced many forms of literature, such as poetry and drama.

Science

Greek scientists first came up with many ideas that have since been proved correct. They were disciplined thinkers and wanted all their ideas to be confirmed by proof—just like modern scientists.

Gods and Goddesses
see page 16

The ancient Greeks worshiped many gods and goddesses, each of whom were believed to help people with different aspects of daily life. The beautiful Artemis, shown here, protected women during childbirth.

Who were the ancient Greeks?

The ancient Greeks lived about 2,500 years ago in the Mediterranean lands of modern Greece and Turkey. Their splendid civilization developed in dozens of self-governing cities around the region, each with its own government, culture, and distinct identity. Many of their ideas about government, knowledge, science, and art became examples to be followed for future generations.

Art

The ancient Greeks built magnificent temples, many of which are still standing. They also made statues and painted vases that tell stories about their gods and goddesses or about daily life.

Democracy
see page 15

The vase painting on the left shows men in Athens voting. Not everyone was allowed to vote in ancient Athens; women and slaves were excluded.

The Cyclades Islands

One of the earliest civilizations developed on the Cyclades Islands. The people of the Cyclades had a rich culture but they left no written records, so we know very little about them. They did leave a lot of beautiful statues, mainly showing women and musicians.

Head carved by people of the Cyclades Islands.

This ornate drinking cup was found at a palace on the island of Crete.

The Mycenaeans

The warlike Mycenaean people conquered the Minoans on Crete in about 1450 BC. Their civilization consisted of a number of small kingdoms, each centered on a citadel, or fortified hilltop town. The great poet Homer (see page 10) told the story of how the mighty Mycenaean soldiers won a great victory against the Trojans during the Trojan War.

The Mycenae soldiers built a hu horse, hid inside it, a left it so that th enemies would find and bring it inside th city. During the nig the Mycenaeans car out and attacked t city of Tr

The Minoans

The Minoans, named after the legendary King Minos, lived on the island of Crete. Their civilization was made up of many small states centered around palaces and ruled by kings. The palaces were surrounded by villages and farms. The Minoans were superb craftspeople and sailors and traded widely.

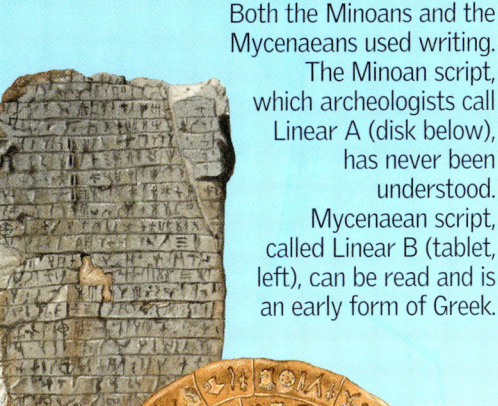

Both the Minoans and the Mycenaeans used writing. The Minoan script, which archeologists call Linear A (disk below), has never been understood. Mycenaean script, called Linear B (tablet, left), can be read and is an early form of Greek.

Before the Greeks

Greek civilization did not just suddenly appear. Other cultures had flourished in the region for thousands of years. The two main early Greek civilizations were those of the Minoans and the Mycenaeans. The Minoans lived on the island of Crete, while the Mycenaeans occupied both Crete and mainland Greece. Both were very advanced, with organized governments and armies, writing systems, and wide trade links.

Timeline

Although real-life history does not divide itself neatly into exact periods, it can be useful to look at some general dates. This timeline shows the main civilizations and periods in Greek history.

1) Cycladic civilization (3000–2000 BC)
2) Minoan civilization (2300–1450 BC)
3) Mycenaean civilization (1650–1200 BC)
4) The Greek "Dark Age" (1200–900 BC)
5) The Archaic period (900–480 BC)
6) The Classical period (480–334 BC)
7) The Hellenistic period (334–30 BC)

This painted centaur (half man, half horse) was buried in a tomb in about 950 BC.

The Dark Age

Mycenaean Greece ended abruptly in about 1200 BC. Little is known about the downfall of the Mycenaeans and the time after the collapse of their civilization. Historians have called this time the "Dark Age." It was probably a time of unrest and migration. Even so, recent studies show that some rich and well-organized cities, such as the port city of Lefkandi, existed even then.

The best early potters and painters came from Athens. This vase shows the twin gods Castor and Pollux on horseback.

Pottery

Before the Archaic period, pottery was mainly decorated with geometric designs and patterns. Then painters began decorating vases with human figures, animals, and scenes from Homer's poems. Artists decorated cups, olive oil jars, water jars, and bowls used for mixing wine and water.

Sculpture

Greek sculptors began carving stone and marble to create life-size statues of the gods and noble people. Archaic sculptors carved elegant and graceful figures. The smiling expression on some figures, known as the "Archaic smile" give the figures a charming appearance.

Homer

The most famous Greek poet is Homer. He lived during the 8th or 9th century BC and composed the *Iliad* and the *Odyssey*. These two famous long poems about Greek gods and heroes became an important part of Greek culture and identity. They were retold by traveling entertainers and passed down to each generation by word of mouth. They were only written down many years later.

According to tradition, Homer was blind. Some believe that he may have been a traveling entertainer himself.

Greek sculpture was painted. This example of an Archaic sculpture of a woman still has some traces of paint.

Olympic Games

During the Archaic period many city-states held sporting events as part of religious festivals. The most famous games were the Olympic Games, held at Olympia in honor of the gods Zeus and Hera (see page 16). The festivities also included banquets and award ceremonies for the winners.

This is a detail of a vase which was given as a prize at the Olympic Games. It shows athletes competing in a horse race.

Archaic Times

By the end of the "Dark Age" people had begun to move from small, unprotected villages to fortified palaces. These settlements later developed into city states, or small nations made up of an independent town and its surrounding countryside. During this time, known as the Archaic period, there were many cultural developments, especially in art and literature. Some of the major city states were Athens, Sparta, Corinth, Thebes, and Argos.

City States

City states were surrounded by protective walls. Inside the walls there was a market place called the agora and an acropolis, or a hilltop site where temples were constructed. Each city state had its own government and money. The first coins were made during the Archaic period. They were made of gold and silver and were used to buy things in the agora and for trade with other city states.

Some examples of Greek coins.

Benefits

Farming in many areas of mainland Greece was difficult and wheat fields were too small to satisfy the growing population. Many colonies had good farmland and food from the colonies was sent to the mainland. Some colonies were also rich in natural resources like metals and lumber.

Settlers who migrated to the island of Sicily built magnificent temples like this one, dedicated to the Greek gods.

This vase painting shows a Greek king directing the weighing and storage of herbs at a colony in North Africa.

A Good Start

When a city state decided to set up a new colony a basic plan was followed. First a group of people were selected to migrate to the new colony. Then a leader was chosen to arrange the voyage. He was assisted by officials who distributed the land and by priests who organized religious worship and rituals. Before the voyage however, people sought the advice of an oracle (see page 17).

The colonists who left Greece moved for good. However, not all of the colonists were welcomed by the people already living in the foreign lands.

Magna Graecia

The colonies that were set up along the coast of southern Italy became known as Magna Graecia, or "Greater Greece." The cities of Magna Graecia became important cultural and trading centers.

A temple decoration of the goddess Medusa from Syracuse, one of the biggest colonies in Magna Graecia, founded in about 733 BC.

Greek Culture

The people who moved to the new colonies kept Greek traditions and culture. They continued to do things the same way they were done back in mainland Greece. As a result, Greek language and culture reached many lands and influenced local art, architecture, farming, and religion.

Greek Colonies

During the Archaic period population on mainland Greece increased greatly. In search of new farm land, natural resources, and new trading opportunities, people began to migrate and settle in many areas around the Mediterranean and Black seas. These new settlements, called colonies, became important trading centers, and some even became independent city-states.

This large bronze vase, found in modern-day France, was made by an artisan from Sparta.

The Black Sea

The ancient Greeks began to move eastward, to the area of the Black Sea, as early as 650 BC. Colonies founded in this region provided excellent trading opportunities. The Greeks traded luxury goods like olive oil, wine, and high quality ceramics and jewels for wheat to feed their growing population.

Luxury items made by Greek artisans have been found in the Black Sea area. This detail comes from a golden comb made in the region.

Sparta

Unlike Athens, which had a democratic government, the city state of Sparta was ruled by a small group headed by a king. The laws in Sparta were very strict. Spartan men were expected to become brave soldiers in service of the state, ready to fight at a moment's notice. Women had the task of raising strong and healthy children. Sports were widely encouraged, even for women, and favored over the arts.

This vase shows a fierce competition between Spartan wrestlers.

Athens

Athens grew into a great cultural center during the Classical period. Some of the greatest Greek thinkers, writers, artists, and politicians came from Athens. As the leader of a group of city states that joined together to fight off foreign invasions Athens became a rich and powerful state.

One of Athens' greatest leaders was Pericles. He improved the city's roads, port, and agora.

Classical Greece

During the Classical period the two leading city states, Athens and Sparta, became great rivals. Athens became the world's first democratic state while Sparta became a mighty military power. Many aspects of daily life in these two cities were different. The agora, in the heart of Athens, was a daily meeting place where men shopped and caught up on the latest gossip and political events. In Sparta, sporting events stole the show.

The Agora

The agora, located in the center of the city or near the port, was full of shops where craftspeople and merchants sold their goods and services. Important monuments and state buildings, such as archives, as well as race tracks, were located in the agora. The agora in Athens had a monument dedicated to its heroes which also served as a public notice-board.

This vase painting shows a blacksmith's workshop in the agora.

Society

In ancient Greece the family unit was the most important part of society. Households were made up of both family members and slaves. Every member's role was well-defined. Men had active roles in public life, while women were bound to the home, raising children and keeping house. Slaves served and obeyed their masters.

Women were not given any decision-making responsibilities. Fathers, brothers, or husbands were in charge.

Bronze statue of a slave boy cleaning a boot. Slaves were people who lost their freedom when their land was conquered by the Greeks.

Democracy

Citizens in Athens had the right to elect their own government leaders and were free to express their own opinions. However, only male Greek landowners were considered citizens. Foreigners, women, and slaves had no say in government and were excluded from public life.

Athenian citizens met at assemblies where government matters were discussed. Citizens voted on important decisions such as the passing of new laws.

Worship at the Temple

Priests and priestesses were in charge of supervising rituals and taking care of the temples.

Religious worship involved prayer and the making of offerings, such as wine, milk, or sweets. Altars stood outside each temple so that rituals could be celebrated in the open air where everyone could see and take part. Inside the temple stood a statue of the god or goddess to whom it was dedicated. Greek temples always faced east-west, in alignment with the sun.

The All-Athens Festival was celebrated in June each year. A great procession was held as the people of Athens carried a new woolen robe for the statue of Athena on the Acropolis.

Gods and Goddesses

The Greeks worshiped many gods and goddesses. The 12 most important ones were believed to live in a big palace on Mount Olympus. Zeus was the chief god. He was married to the goddess Hera. The other goddesses were Artemis (goddess of the hunt, nature, and childbirth), Athena (goddess of war and crafts, and of Athens), Aphrodite (goddess of love and beauty), Demeter (goddess of agriculture), and Hestia (goddess of home and family.) Besides Zeus, the male gods were Apollo (god of law, music, poetry, and dance), Ares (god of war), Poseidon (god of the sea, earthquakes, and horses), Hephaestus (god of fire and art), and Hermes (god of trade).

Feast Days

Many feast days and festivals were held during the year. There were farming festivals, days to remember the dead, celebrations for the gods, and more. The two main festivals in Athens were the All-Athens Festival, and the City Dionysia, when plays were staged and poetry read.

Oracles

The Greeks went to shrines called oracles to ask questions about the future. The answers to the questions were interpreted by priestesses who gave the questioner their reply. The oracle of Apollo at Delphi was one of the most famous shrines.

Religion

Religion was an important part of daily life. Decisions, including government ones such as whether to go to war or not, and personal ones like who to marry, were only made after consulting with a god or goddess through an oracle. Every village and town was dedicated to one or more gods. Athens, for example, was dedicated to the goddess Athena and everyone had to worship her. Greek stories about their origins and gods were preserved as myths.

Dish showing a man consulting the oracle at Delphi.

Bronze statue of Zeus, god of justice and lord of the sky. When angry he threw thunderbolts.

A golden statue of Athena stood inside her temple, the Parthenon (see page 18).

The top of this building is supported by columns in the shape of beautiful women.

Doric column

Ionic column

Corinthian column

Columns

Columns not only supported buildings, but they also were an important decorative element. Greek architects created many designs, like the ones shown above, to embellish capitals (the top parts of columns).

The Human Body

Greek sculptors of the Classical period represented the human body in a realistic way. They studied the relationship between the parts of the body to give each part the right dimensions. They also studied how the body moves and could create sculptures of muscular athletes.

Architecture

The Parthenon is one of the greatest works of Greek architecture. This Athenian temple was built in honor of Athena on the acropolis, the highest point of the city. The architects of the Parthenon designed the building so that each of the architectural elements, such as its columns, were at equal distance from each other. This created a sense of order and harmony both inside and outside the building. The temple was also decorated with colors and relief sculpture.

The statue of the *Discus Thrower* show muscles of the the body at wor

This is how the Parthenon may have looked when it was built.

Sculpture

The Greek sculptors created works with a flat background, called reliefs, to decorate the surfaces of temples and other important buildings. Sculptors created figures and fantastic scenes which seemed to emerge from the buildings' surfaces.

This horse's head is a detail of a relief that was made to decorate the Parthenon.

Painting

Most of the wall and panel paintings that Greek painters created have been destroyed over the centuries. However, fine examples of Greek painting can be found on vases. Painters depicted a variety of subjects, including scenes from everyday life and myths. These scenes tell us a lot about how the ancient Greeks lived.

This black-figure vase painting shows two heroes, Ajax and Achilles, playing a board game.

Art and Architecture

Art and architecture are perhaps the most studied and admired aspects of Greek culture. The Greeks applied new rules to art which were based on a close study of the natural world around them. They created realistic statues, harmonious buildings, and beautiful paintings which brought the stories they depicted to life.

Vase painters from Athens became famous for their skills. Some signed their names on their creations.

Vase Painting

At first vases were decorated with black figures and details were added by cutting into the surface. Then, during the Classical period, new techniques were developed to make the paintings seem more realistic. Artists created red-figure vases. Vase painters drew the scene on the vase and then colored only the background and details. When the vase was baked, the uncolored parts turned red.

Bronze war helmet.

An early one-level warship, called a penteconter.

A bireme, showing its two levels and 56 oars.

A Greek soldier in battle gear.

Warriors and War

The Greeks fought frequent wars, sometimes among their own city states and sometimes against outside enemies, such as the Persians. Many city states had large armies and fleets of deadly warships. Alexander the Great was the most famous Greek warrior. He conquered one of the largest empires the world has ever known.

Soldiers

Greek foot soldiers, called hoplites, wore heavy armor, and carried a sword, a shield, and a long spear. Soldiers from Athens provided their own weapons and gear. Only the wealthy could afford horses.

In battle, soldiers massed together in rows so that if one was killed the man behind stepped into his place.

Warships

The first Greek warships, called pentecontors, had just a few oarsmen on a single level. Then the bireme was invented. This had 56 oarsmen sitting on two levels. Light and fast, this ship was also a favorite with pirates. But it was the trireme, first built at Corinth in about 700 BC, that became the most important ship of Greek navies. With 170 rowers on three levels, it was both powerful and fast.

This detail of a mosaic shows Alexander the Great riding into battle.

Leaders

Alexander the Great was a powerful leader who became emperor in 336 BC, when he was just 20 years old. Within 10 years he created an empire that stretched from Greece to northern India.

fleet of triremes being ...wed into battle.

Major Wars

The Greek city states were united against their powerful neighbors, the Persians, in a series of wars that raged off and on for much of the 5th century BC. But later, between 431–404 BC, the city states were divided and aligned either with Athens or Sparta in an internal struggle known as the Peloponnesian War.

Plays and Actors

Plays told stories of people and the gods. There were three kinds of plays: plays with sad endings, called tragedies; plays with happy endings called comedies; and amusing plays in which men dressed as satyrs, forest creatures with the ears, legs, and horns of a goat, filled the chorus. All of the actors were men, even those who played the roles of women. Each actor wore a mask which had facial expressions to match the part he was playing.

An actor in costume, with h mask in hand, prepares for a performance.

The mask above was worn in a tragedy, the one on the right was worn in a comedy.

The Theater

Huge theaters were built to hold large crowds. The seats were arranged in a semicircle and faced the orchestra, a circular floor in the center of the theater where the chorus performed. The chorus was a group of actors who played music and recited poems during the play. The stage was behind the orchestra and was part of a building used by actors to prepare for the performance.

Sports

The ancient Greeks took sports seriously. Sports were not only a big part of young men's education, but they were also tied to religious festivals. At stadiums spectators enjoyed watching athletes compete. Gifted athletes were highly regarded.

The Greeks thought sports were an excellent way to develop their minds and bodies.

Music

Music was a big part of everyday life in ancient Greece. Religious feast days, banquets, and theater all involved music. Music even accompanied the daily routines of manual workers and soldiers in training.

A musician instructs two of his pupils how to play the lyre.

This child's toy, of a goose and rider, is made from baked clay. Geese, ducks, and small birds were popular pets.

Theater
and Entertainment

In their free time the Greeks participated in sports, played music, held banquets, and enjoyed plays at the theater. The earliest performances were part of religious festivals dedicated to the god Dionysus. Since most public functions were for men only, women spent their time in private quarters with children, enjoying games and lively conversation.

Games

The ancient Greeks played many games of chance. One of the most popular pastimes was the game of knucklebones, which was similar to the modern game of jacks. Players had to throw game pieces in the air and catch them with the backs of their hands. Game pieces were made from sheep or cattle bones.

Knucklebones was a popular game with women.

All men were required to go to the theater. Poor people who were not able to buy their own tickets were given money so that they too could attend.

Education

Boys attended school from the age of seven. Students learned to read and write and master the rules of grammar. The major subjects were literature, sports, and music. Girls were taught at home. They were trained to become good wives. Few girls learned to read and write and play instruments.

Since schools were private, not all families could afford to send their children to school.

Doctors studied plants for their healing abilities. Herbs were used to make medicines.

This carving shows a doctor, attended by a nurse, treating a patient.

Knowledge

The ancient Greeks gave the world their love of knowledge, their curiosity, and their persistent search for truth. Greek doctors studied the human body and tried to cure illness. Great thinkers tried to answer questions about human behavior, judging right from wrong. Scientists, mathematicians, astrologers, and engineers all worked to improve conditions of everyday life.

Medicine

Greek doctors became famous for their ability to perform surgery and make medicines. Unlike the doctors before their time, Greek doctors began to study how the body worked to find cures instead of relying on magic.

Inventions

Greek inventors created all sorts of machines and devices to help them carry out more difficult tasks. They invented a tool to keep time, steam-powered engines, and pumps. They also invented a machine which used energy from a burning fire to open large temple doors.

Anaximander invented the sundial, a tool used to measure time.

The Greeks used the abacus to make calculations.

Mathematics

The Greeks discovered that mathematical rules could be applied to many aspects of the natural world. They used math to compose music, calculate and measure distances, study the Earth and the stars, and many other things in the universe. Math was one of the most important subjects studied at school.

Pythagoras was both a philosopher and mathematician.

Philosophers loved to share their ideas and debate with others.

Philosophy

The word philosophy comes from the Greek word meaning "love of wisdom." The ancient Greek philosophers studied the origins and nature of the world. They asked questions about the nature of people and their behavior. They tried to find explanations for why things happened and what caused them.

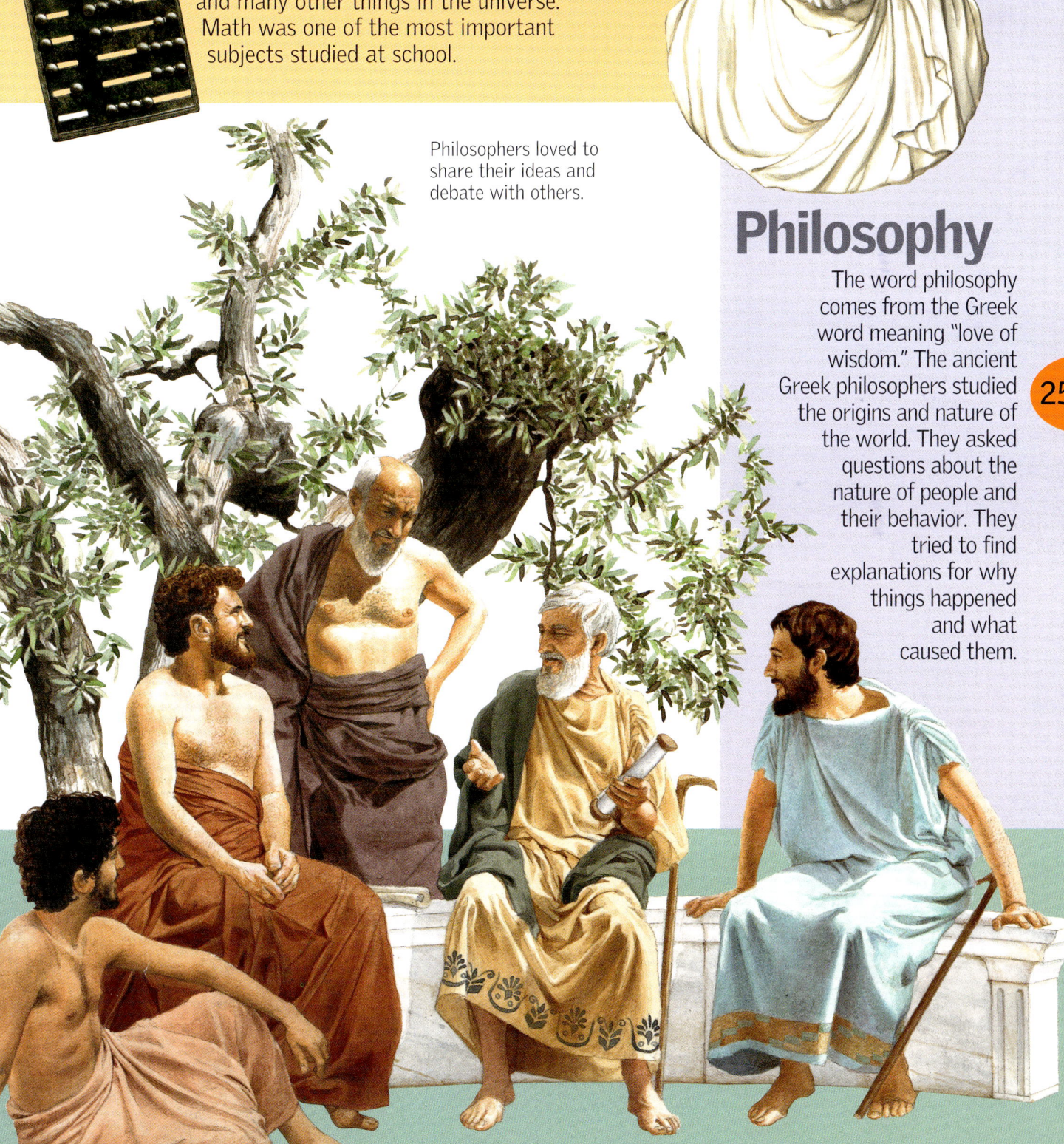

25

The Greek Diet

A typical meal consisted of bread and fruit, with herbs and honey. Meat was only eaten on special occasions and only the rich could afford it. People who lived near the sea ate fish, but even fish was expensive. Lentil soup was a favorite among the poor.

The wealth[y] sipped the[ir] beverages [in] fancy cups, many in decorative animal shape[s]

This decorative bowl was made to serve fish. Food preparation became an art. Cook books and poems were written about food.

Dinner Parties

Wealthy Greek men participated in dinner parties which were an occasion to eat a good meal and enjoy the company of friends. They ate leaning back on couches and were served by young boys and women who also provided musical entertainment. Some dinner parties were more formal where men discussed serious topics, such as politics.

Large pots called kraters were used to mix wine with water.

Farming

A farmer's life was not an easy one. They was a lot of work to be done all year round. The heavy fall rainfalls and the hot dry summers often damaged crops. Farmers had to carefully plan the right time to plant their seeds.

To prepare the soil for planting, farmers used wooden machines pulled by oxen or mules, called plows, to turn over the land.

Crops

Greek farmers grew many kinds of fruits, vegetables, and different kinds of nuts. Farmers were not able to grow large quantities of wheat because of the poor soil condition. Barley, however, was more plentiful. Olives were an important crop. When grain supply was low the Greeks traded olive oil for wheat.

Food and Farming

The ancient Greeks made the best of what the land provided. Their food supply came not only from farming, but from fishing, hunting, and trade. Although Greek farmers kept many animals, the typical diet for both rich and poor alike did not include much meat. The most important foods were cereals, cheese, vegetables, and fish. Almost every home had olive oil and wine on the table.

Large amounts of wheat were imported from the colonies.

Animals

Sheep and goats were raised by many farmers for their milk and wool. Pigs and chickens were kept too, for meat and eggs. Large animals, such as horses, donkeys, and oxen were put to work, pulling plows in the fields. Bees were also kept to make honey, which was mixed with water to make a tasty beverage.

Milk from sheep and goats had to be used immediately before it turned sour. It was used to make cheese which could be stored for a long time.

Men's Clothing

All clothes, for both men and women, were made of rectangular pieces of cloth wrapped around the body or held together by pins. Men wore long or short tunics which were fastened on both sides or only on one. Over this garment they draped a large piece of woolen cloth. Slaves wore very simple, short tunics which were tied at the waist leaving one shoulder bare.

A citizen, on the left, wears a large piece of woolen cloth draped over a long tunic, while a worker, on the right, wears a shorter tunic.

Clothing
and Jewelry

Greek craftspeople were able to make elaborate jewels like this gold earring by pouring melted gold into clay molds.

Jewelry

Most men did not wear much jewelry. They wore signet rings which were used to seal letters. Wealthy women wore necklaces, ornate earrings, bracelets, and crowns. Jewelry was made from a range of materials including metals such as gold, copper, and silver, and baked clay. Children wore good luck charms for protection.

Although clothing styles and customs were different from region to region, the ancient Greeks took good care of their bodies. Greek men bathed in public bath houses, and those fortunate enough to have a bathtub, bathed at home. Clothing and hairstyle told a lot about a person's social status and where they came from. Putting on jewelry, as well as perfume and make-up were everyday routines for many wealthy people.

Women used bronze mirrors like this one to apply make-up.

Perfume and Make-up

Both men and women used perfume. There were many kinds of scents, made mostly from flowers and spices. Women wore make-up to lighten their faces and make their cheeks and lips rosy. They also wore wore colorful eyeshadow and darkened their eyebrows. Wealthy women were attended by their slaves who helped them to apply make-up and perfume and do their hair.

The most common shoe was the leather sandal.

Weaving

Women spent a large part of their time making cloth. It was made from wool and cotton. Wool was first dyed and then spun into thread before being woven into cloth. Large frames called looms were used to weave thread into large rectangular pieces of cloth which were used to make clothing. Women could make different patterns by weaving threads of varying colors, painting designs, and using special materials, such as gold thread.

Women's Clothing

Women wore a large, long rectangular article of clothing that was pinned at the shoulders and tied at the waist. It could have long sleeves or no sleeves at all. The most common fabric was wool while the finest and most expensive clothes were made from linen.

Weaving, an important women's task, was done standing up at the loom.

The most expensive dye was purple, which was made from shells. Insects and minerals were also used to make other colors.

Hairstyles

Hairstyles varied from region to region. In Sparta, children's heads were shaved while in Athens only slaves had shaved heads. Men in Athens had short, simple hairstyles, while their Spartan neighbors wore their hair long. All women, except slaves, had long hair. Women wore their hair up, tied up with nets and ribbons, in buns, pony tails, or braids. Many women wore hair pieces.

Ribbons were used to tie hair up. Earrings were the favorite jewelry of wealthy women.

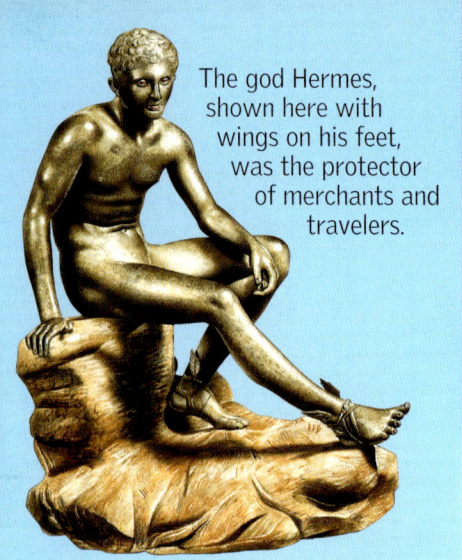

The god Hermes, shown here with wings on his feet, was the protector of merchants and travelers.

Ports

Ports were a vital part of Greek cities like Athens which depended on trade for a major part of its food supply. The port of Athens, Piraeus, was protected with strong walls which connected it to the city. Many people, especially foreign traders, settled in the port.

Traded Goods

The Greeks depended on trade to obtain materials they needed such as metals, foodstuffs, and lumber. Goods were transported by sea since the mountainous land made travel difficult. Colonies were excellent bases for merchants and travelers and allowed the Greeks to compete with foreign traders.

Horse-shaped perfume bottle from Rhodes. Perfumes were imported from the East.

Trade and Influence

The Greeks traded crafted goods and farm produce far and wide and the city states grew wealthy. However, the greatest Greek export was their way of life and love of learning and the arts which reached all corners of the known world. Even today, elements of Greek culture can be found in politics, medicine, sports, and much more.

Hellenistic Culture

The Classical period was followed by the Hellenistic period. During this time Alexander the Great ruled over the Greek world. He conquered many lands and spread Greek culture into North Africa and Western Asia. Many non-Greek peoples followed Greek customs and spoke Greek.

A portrait sculpture of Alexander the Great when he was a young boy.

Influence Today

Greek culture is a part of many aspects of modern life. The modern Western alphabet is believed to have come from the Greek alphabet. Also, Greek traditions are still alive today. The Olympic Games bring people together to celebrate the accomplishments of great athletes.

Many ideas the Greeks had about science have been proven true. The fact that all objects are made up of small particles called atoms was originally a Greek idea.

In the late 19th century the Olympic Games were started up again. Like in ancient times, an Olympic flame is lit in Olympia. The flame is then carried all the way to the site of the games.

Successful merchants had their own ships and became very wealthy. However they risked losing large cargos to shipwrecks and pirates.

The Greek Example

Not only are the ancient Greeks studied in schools and universities but their ideas about good moral behavior are still respected today. For example, doctors make a promise, called the Hippocratic oath, named after the Greek doctor Hippocrates. They promise to treat patients to the best of their ability and to share knowledge about medicine with others.

Above: Hippocrates traveled all over the Greek world practicing and teaching medicine.

Index

Achilles 19
acropolis 11, 18
actors 22
agora 11, 14
Ajax 19
Alexander the Great 20, 21, 31
Anaximander 24
animals 27
Archaic period 9, 11, 13
architecture 13, 18–19
Argos 11
art 13, 18–19,
Athens 6, 7, 11, 14, 15, 16, 17, 19, 20, 21, 29, 30

Black Sea 13

chorus 22
city states 11, 14, 20, 21, 30
Classical period 9, 14, 18, 19, 31
clothing and jewelry 28–29
colonies 12–13
colonists 12
Corinth 11, 21
Crete 8, 9
Cyclades Islands 8
Cycladic civilization 9

"Dark Age" 9, 11
Delphi 17
democracy 6, 15
Discus Thrower 18
drama (*see also* plays) 7

Earth 25
education 24
entertainment 22–23

farming 12, 13, 26–27
feast days and festivals 17, 23
    – All-Athens Festival 16, 17
    – City Dionysia 17
food 26–27

games 23
gods and goddesses 6, 7, 12, 16
    – Aphrodite 16
    – Apollo 16, 17
    – Ares 16
    – Artemis 7, 16
    – Athena 16, 17, 18
    – Castor 10
    – Demeter 16
    – Dionysus 23
    – Hephaestus 16
    – Hera 11, 16
    – Hermes 16, 30
    – Hestia 16
    – Medusa 13
    – Pollux 10
    – Poseidon 16
    – Zeus 11, 16, 17
Greece 7, 9, 12, 13, 15. 21, 31
Greek language 9, 13, 31

Hellenistic period 9, 31
Hippocrates 31
history 7
Homer 8, 10
    – *Iliad* 10
    – *Odyssey* 10
hoplites 20

India 21
Italy 13

knowledge 7, 24–25

Lefkandi 9
literature 7, 24

Magna Graecia 13
masks 22
mathematics 25
medicine 24, 30, 31
Mediterranean Sea 13
Minoan civilization 9
Minoan script (Linear A) 9
Minoans 9
Minos, King 9
Mount Olympus 16
music 22, 23, 24
musicians 6, 8, 23
Mycenaean civilization 9
Mycenaean script (Linear B) 9
Mycenaeans 8, 9

North Africa 12, 31

Olympia 11, 31
Olympic Games 11, 31
oracles 12, 17

painting 19

Parthenon 17, 18, 19
Peloponnesian War 21
perfume and make-up 28
Pericles 14
Persians 20, 21
philosophy 7, 25
Piraeus 30
plays 17, 22, 23
poetry 7, 17
ports 9, 30
pottery 10
priests and priestesses 12, 16
Pythagoras 25

religion 13, 16–17

Sicily 12
sculpture 10, 18, 19
slaves 7, 15, 28, 29
soldiers (*see also* warriors *and* hoplites) 8, 14, 20, 23
Sparta 11, 14, 21, 29
sports 14, 22, 23, 24, 30
Syracuse 13

temples 7, 16
theaters 22–23
Thebes 11
Turkey 7
trade and trading 13, 11, 27, 30–31
Trojans 8
Trojan War 8
Troy 8

warriors 6, 20–21
wars 20–21
warships 21
    – biremes 20, 21
    – pentecontors 20, 21
    – triremes 20, 21
weaving 29
Western Asia 31